Waves

Stephen Clark

Making Waves

Amber Lane Press

All rights whatsoever in this play are strictly reserved
and application for professional performance
should be made before rehearsals begin to:
Judy Daish Associates Ltd
2 St Charles Place
London W10 6EG

Application for amateur performance
should be made before rehearsals begin to:
Samuel French Ltd
52 Fitzroy Street
London W1T 5JR

No performance may be given unless a licence has been obtained.

First published in 2004 by
Amber Lane Press Ltd
Church Street, Charlbury, Oxon OX7 3PR
Telephone: 01608 810024
E-mail: info@amberlanepress.co.uk

Printed and bound by
Creative Print and Design Group, Harmondsworth and Ebbw Vale

ISBN: 1 872868 38 X

Thank you:

To Laura and Alan for asking for a story.
To the RNLI, the crews and their partners
for giving me the beginnings of the story.
To Brian, Maggie and Meredith
for reading and re-reading the story.
To Danny for nurturing the story.
And to Oscar for being there
when the story was finally told.

The Writing of *Making Waves*

I'd just moved to Brighton to a flat overlooking the sea. It wasn't an accident. I'd run away to the sea. And of course Scarborough is on the sea and I thought perhaps this play could provide a chance to explore why I'd run away to it. It's the edge of the land, of safety; the beach provides golden memories of childhood days and yet it's also the beginning of extreme danger. We come from the sea and yet it claims lives at its merest whim. It's enticing, beautiful, violent and terrifying. But to explore all this I needed an angle.

Whilst staring at the sea I wondered about the local life-boat-men. I thought if anyone knows about the sea and its power, it would be them. So I rang the RNLI and they kindly put me in touch with some of the local lifeboat stations and their crews. I talked to the men about the challenges, the risks, the bond between them, the boats, the sea . . . and it was all fascinating. These men are heroes. We live on an island and they patrol the edges, fighting for lives, keeping us safe no matter how daft or unlucky we are. But despite the wealth of stories I could find no conflict . . . the essential ingredient for any drama. But then I met their wives and girlfriends . . . Suddenly the play became clear. The demands the boat makes on the men is immense . . . they have to be trained, they have to be ready, they choose to risk their lives for others . . . therefore it also makes demands on their families. As I talked to the women it became clear that they are proud, genuinely proud, of their men, but that the demands are not without their consequences . . .

Stephen Clark
Brighton, 2003

Characters

RUTH TANNER, 49, the mother of the family

MIKE TANNER, 54, coxswain of the Teesmouth Lifeboat
and father of the family

SAM TANNER, 28, their elder son,
a website developer working in New York

LUKE TANNER, 24, their younger son,
a carpenter by trade, and a volunteer lifeboat crewman

JO TANNER, 19, their daughter, works in the local pub

HELEN, 22, Luke's girlfriend,
works at a wildlife sanctuary

The Tanner family live in Teesmouth,
a town somewhere on the northeast coast of England.

Making Waves is set in the present and takes place
over a period of nine days during the month of October.
The action takes place in three locations:

1. The Tanners' kitchen.
It is a basic but well-kept room and is the heart of the house.
The main focus is the kitchen table,
which is big enough to seat six.

2. Luke's workshop.
This is an old, weathered, wooden building
that was once a boathouse. Luke is in the process
of converting it to a properly equipped carpentry workshop.

3. The beach: a strip of coastline
close to where the Tanners live.

Making Waves was first presented on Wednesday 30 April
2003 at the Stephen Joseph Theatre, Scarborough.
It was directed by Daniel Slater with the following cast:

MIKE ... Geoff Leesley
RUTH ... Charlie Hardwick
SAM ... James Weaver
LUKE ... Neil Grainger
JO ... Alison Mac
HELEN ... Niky Wardley

Designed by Francis O'Connor
Lighting Design by James Farncombe
Sound Design by Ben Vickers

The cast for the development workshop was:

MIKE ... John Bett
RUTH ... Sarah Collier
SAM ... Nick Reding
LUKE ... Matt Hodgson
JO ... Sarah Sansom
HELEN ... Megan Fisher

Development workshop funded by:
The Cameron Mackintosh Foundation
The Peggy Ramsay Foundation
The Really Useful Group

Thank you to Bruno Beloff for advice on the world of
website developers.

ACT ONE

*While the audience are entering and settling down there
is a very low level SFX of the sea playing in the back-
ground. In the last two minutes before the play starts,
the sea slowly gets louder and louder until it is unbear-
able. It then suddenly stops to reveal the dull thumping
of music from upstairs: 'Blow My Whistle Baby' by DJ
Alligator.*

Scene One

The kitchen. Tuesday. Late afternoon.

*At the same time as the sea SFX stop, the lights fade up
on a kitchen table.* RUTH *is carefully setting the table,
laid with a spotless white tablecloth. There are even
serviettes. She is making a special effort. When she has
finished laying the table she carefully arranges a plate
of sandwiches in the middle, taking great care that they
look perfect. She becomes more aware of the thumping
music from upstairs. She looks upwards in despair.*

RUTH: Jo!

> [*No response. The music keeps playing.*]

Jo!

> [*Still no response.* RUTH *goes over to the door and
> screams.*]

Jo!

[*The music stops. Relieved,* RUTH *goes back to the table.* JO *enters from the inside door. She is clearly very pissed off.*]

JO: What!

RUTH: It's five o'clock.

JO: So?

RUTH: So, your brother'll be here soon . . .

JO: But he's not here yet.

RUTH: No. But he's due any minute.

JO: I've taken the night off work, haven't I? What's the problem?

RUTH: You haven't seen him for five years! Your dad and Luke are out on the bloody boat, and I want us to be ready when he gets here!

JO: I've been ready for five years. It's not my fault Sam hasn't bothered coming home.

[*The phone rings.* RUTH *picks it up.*]

RUTH: Hello? [*listens for a while*] Right. Thanks for letting us know.

[*She puts the phone down.* JO *is looking at her, puzzled, worried.*]

That was Sam's friend. Sam's been offered a new job and he's cancelled the trip.

JO: [*hugely disappointed*] You what! You're joking, aren't you?

RUTH: I'm sorry, love. Maybe next year . . . who knows . . . ?

JO: [*hurt*] He's not coming home? After all this time? If he leaves it much longer he won't recognise us.

RUTH: [*smiles*] Actually it was the catalogue. My new skirt's in the post.

JO: I s'pose you think you're funny!

RUTH: [*still smiling*] Not half as funny as how stroppy you've been all week. What you so scared of? He's just our Sam.

JO: He'd better bloody be . . .

RUTH: Last time you saw him he was your hero. Don't be too hard on him.

[HELEN *enters. During the next dialogue she goes to put her coat on the back of a chair but* RUTH *grabs it, anxious that everything's perfect.*]

HELEN: Hiya. Not too late to help, am I?

RUTH: Helen! It's never too late to help. And Luke's back safe. Should be here soon.

HELEN: Aye. He rang me.

RUTH: He's a good lad.

HELEN: Specially when he's on dry land.

LUKE: [*offstage*] Hello!

RUTH: Talk of the devil.

[LUKE *enters. He's still quite 'adrenalined'. He looks round at the kitchen, as if it were all for him.*]

LUKE: Aw, Mam . . . you shouldn't have bothered . . .

[MIKE *enters.*]

RUTH: Nowt wrong with making a bit of an effort. Now I don't want you tramping those boots all over the floor. Why didn't you take them off outside?

[*She grabs* LUKE's *coat as he takes it off.* LUKE *sits on one of the chairs and starts pulling his boots off.*]

MIKE: S'not like the bloody Queen's coming . . .

[HELEN *goes over to* LUKE *and helps him with a boot.* RUTH *grabs* MIKE's *coat as he takes it off and exits with the three coats to the hallway.*]

LUKE: Thank you . . . I could get used to this!

HELEN: I wouldn't. Just pleased to see you safe. How was
          it?

          [MIKE *sits down and takes his boots off while* LUKE
          speaks.]

LUKE: Bloody amazing! A fishing boat. Norwegian. Got
          them all off . . . well . . . except the cat. You should
          have seen Dad. He held us next to that boat like
          bloody glue. God knows how. Waves rolling over us!
          One of the crew was afraid to jump but still he held
          us there. Best bloody coxswain in the country!

MIKE: Now, Luke . . . there's no need for stories. A day's
          work, that's all.

LUKE: And then just as we were pulling away, this massive
          wave –

MIKE: I said that's enough!

          [LUKE *is a bit hurt, especially in front of* HELEN.
          RUTH *enters.*]

RUTH: [*to* MIKE] Look . . . you've got mud on the floor – that'll
          have to be cleaned up. And get those boots out of
          here before you make any more mess.

          [*She goes to get a mop.* HELEN *sees that* LUKE *is still
          embarrassed and hugs him.*]

HELEN: It's good to see you. I've missed you.

LUKE: Since this morning?

HELEN: I *always* miss you . . .

          [LUKE *smiles and they kiss.* RUTH *returns with the
          mop and sees that no one has moved.*]

RUTH: Or do I have to set a bloody maroon off to get you
          into action?

          [*She starts to wipe the floor.*]

MIKE: [*to* LUKE] I don't know why you think *you* can stand there like a lump of lard. Get yourself ready or your mam'll never cheer up.

LUKE: [*with a hint of sarcasm*] Aye aye, cox'n.

[LUKE *and* MIKE *exit to the hallway to put their boots away.*]

RUTH: I just want everything to be ready for when he gets here. It's a long flight and he'll be tired.

JO: Mam . . . you haven't stopped all week . . . it *is* ready . . .

[RUTH *looks around, looking for faults, but sees that* JO *is right. She smiles ruefully and sits down heavily.*]

RUTH: Guess it'll never be good enough . . .

JO: Do you think he'll bring us presents?

RUTH: Just him being here'll be enough of a present.

[LUKE *and* MIKE *return.* LUKE *takes his place at the table but* MIKE *stands back, ill at ease.*]

JO: He must be *loaded* by now. Surely he'll bring something.

HELEN: I wonder if he's got an American accent.

LUKE: Sounds like it on the phone.

MIKE: He'd better get rid of that sharp enough.

HELEN: Do we know if he's seeing anyone?

LUKE: Why?

HELEN: Just wondered. If he's that successful and everything . . .

[SAM *enters unseen and hovers in the doorway. He is carrying a Samsonite suitcase, a laptop bag and an expensive-looking carrier bag.*]

RUTH: He's never mentioned anyone special. But you never know with Sam. I get the feeling he doesn't tell us everything.

HELEN: You know I can't even remember what he looks like. Didn't he wear glasses?

JO: For two weeks. Then he got contacts. He always was a vain bugger.

RUTH: Jo! I won't have you talking about your brother like that.

[MIKE *catches sight of* SAM *in the doorway.* SAM *looks back at him. Neither of them says anything.*]

JO: He spent longer in the bathroom than me.

LUKE: *No one* spends longer in the bathroom than you. If it were an Olympic event, you'd be a national hero.

[RUTH *notices* MIKE.]

RUTH: And what you staring at?

[*She looks towards where* MIKE *is looking. She sees* SAM *and stops. A beat.*]

Sam!

[*Everyone looks round.*]

SAM: [*with an American accent*] Hi!

RUTH: How long have you been standing there?

SAM: Not long . . . just remembering the joys of family life . . .

RUTH: Well, come in! It's your home and all!

[*She moves to him and hugs him.*]

Look at you! You've lost weight.

SAM: I had to. When I first arrived they called me the Yorkshire Pudding.

[*He goes over to* LUKE *and holds out his hand. They shake hands but then* SAM *pulls him into a hug.*]

Good to see you, little brother.

LUKE: Good to see you too, Sam.

[SAM *goes over to* JO.]

SAM: Well, *you've* changed.

[SAM *kisses her on each cheek, which is a first for* JO.]

Last time I saw you, you were all spotty and moody and always playing your music too loud.

RUTH: Yes . . . well . . . the spots have gone . . .

[*A beat.* SAM *turns to* HELEN.]

SAM: So you must be Helen. Mum told me Luke had fallen on his feet. But I didn't realise he'd had such a beautiful landing.

[HELEN *is as flattered as she is embarrassed.*]

It's a pleasure to meet you.

HELEN: Actually, we've met quite a lot before . . . I'm Tom's sister . . . little sister as it was then . . .

SAM: The one with braces and pigtails?

HELEN: The very same.

SAM: Isn't growing up a wonderful thing?

[*They look at each other, holding the gaze a tad too long.* SAM *breaks away and holds his hand out to* MIKE. *They shake hands, a very Yorkshire shake.*]

Hello, Dad.

MIKE: Son.

[*A beat.*]

RUTH: Now come on . . . take the weight off your pegs . . . you must be very tired . . .

[*They all begin to take their places at the table.*]

SAM: Bushed. I made a big presentation to some potential backers just before I came. Haven't slept for nights.

   [*His chair wobbles. He looks down, confused.*]

JO: It's one of Luke's. He made everything in here. And it all wobbles.

RUTH: If he gets it right, he sells it. If it wobbles, *we* get it.

LUKE: I thought you liked them . . .

RUTH: [*to* SAM] I didn't know when you'd get here so I made some sandwiches to keep us going. But there's a little something in the oven for later. A real family meal.

JO: Oh no . . . not something special, is it?

SAM: Thank you, Mum.

JO: Don't thank her yet. Mam's got into 'multi-cultural cuisines' and if she's cooked you something special, I guarantee you'll end up down the chippie.

RUTH: Mind your tongue, lass.

JO: It's my tongue I'm worried about.

RUTH: There's nowt wrong with trying summat a bit different.

JO: And what is it this time?

RUTH: [*proudly*] Nigerian peanut stew.

JO: [*to* SAM] See you at the chippie.

SAM: It's very kind of you, Mum, but to tell the truth I ate a lot on the plane . . . well . . . there's not much else to do . . . I'm sure a couple of sandwiches'll be more than enough . . .

   [*They all grab a sandwich with gusto, except* RUTH.]

RUTH: So how long are you staying, Sam? I know you're very busy.

SAM: Just till Sunday, I'm afraid. Schedules, deadlines, time-scales, you know how it is.

RUTH: I'm just glad you can manage five days.

SAM: And on Friday I've squeezed in a presentation at the Newcastle Chamber of Commerce. I'm hoping they might put some money in the project next year.

MIKE: But that's your mother's birthday.

SAM: . . . I know. I just thought I'd go say hello while I'm around.

> [*He puts on his best local accent. It comes across as a bit patronising.*]

Play the local-boy card. You know.

MIKE: You don't *sound* like a local boy . . .

SAM: I live in New York. You gotta talk the talk.

RUTH: Well, I think it sounds rather nice.

> [*An uneasy pause.*]

HELEN: So how *is* New York, then?

SAM: It's one long goddam meeting. But it's a positive curve and the prognosis looks better than good.

RUTH: So . . . you're doing well . . .

SAM: Absolutely. I've been pitching some projections to VCs and if I can just centre us in the feeding frenzy we'll be IPO before you can spell NASDAQ.

> [*They all stare at him.*]

> [*to* RUTH] And to celebrate . . . I bought you a present.

> [*He hands* RUTH *the expensive-looking carrier bag.*]

RUTH: For my birthday?

SAM: No . . . for being my mom.

RUTH: Oh Sam . . . you shouldn't have . . .

> [*She carefully takes out the contents of the bag. It is a Donna Karan trouser suit, wrapped in tissue paper. She unwraps it and holds it against herself, thrilled.*]

It's beautiful . . . really lovely . . .

SAM: It's Donna Karan.

RUTH: Donna . . .

JO: Kebab.

SAM: . . . Karan. Everyone who's anyone's wearing it.

RUTH: Oh . . . lovely . . .

SAM: You're gonna look fantastic in it, I just know it.

> [*A beat.*]

RUTH: I nearly forgot!

> [*She suddenly rushes out.*]

JO: [*to* SAM] Now you're here, maybe she'll stop driving us up the wall.

LUKE: I wouldn't bet on it.

> [RUTH *returns with a bottle of champagne.*]

RUTH: Ta-da . . . !

> [*She gives the champagne to* SAM.]

SAM: Champagne!

RUTH: I don't know if it's any good.

JO: We haven't had any champagne since Great Aunt Phyllis died.

> [SAM *laughs.*]

RUTH: Jo! We said we wouldn't tell anyone.

JO: Come on, Mam, Sam hated her as much as we did.

RUTH: Even so . . . you shouldn't speak ill of the dead.

[*A beat.*]

But thank God she is.

[*They all laugh.*]

SAM: So what we doing on your birthday, Mum?

RUTH: We're having a fancy dress do at the Jolly Anchor.

SAM: What? I thought I could take us all for a special meal.

RUTH: No . . . it's a fund-raiser . . . for the RNLI.

SAM: But Mum, it's your fiftieth birthday! I've come all this way to celebrate and you're working!

MIKE: It's for a bloody good cause.

[*Pause.*]

SAM: You'll be needing a bartender, then.

JO: Not if it takes you this long to open a bottle of champagne . . .

[SAM *opens the bottle and start to pour the champagne.*]

SAM: [*to* LUKE] So, how's the business going? You're finally making some money?

LUKE: Aye. Finished a wardrobe for the Richards last week. Paid a grand for it.

SAM: You? A thousand pounds?

LUKE: They wanted it in teak. Pricey stuff.

SAM: Does it wobble?

HELEN: I think it's beautiful.

LUKE: [*to* SAM] I've even found a workshop. The garage is getting too small. It's gonna be mega. Tons of room, loads of light, and just down the road –

JO: – so he can nip back for his dinner.

SAM: Wow! Luke gets a life! And what about you, Jo? Mum said in her letters you're still dreaming about going round the world . . .

JO: And I will. Just you wait. I've been working in the Anchor. Not that it pays much, but I've saved some and maybe next year I'll have enough to get started . . .

SAM: [*sarcastic*] Sounds definite, then . . .

JO: It is! There're some really cheap flights to Thailand . . . I'm hoping to start in Bangkok and work in a bar, then go to Koh Samui for two weeks to go on a scuba diving course, and then work my way down to Kuala Lumpur. Then I'll see how it goes. Maybe I'll even get to Bali.

RUTH: I didn't know everything was so . . . settled . . .

MIKE: Nothing's settled.

[*An awkward pause.* SAM *offers* MIKE *a glass of champagne.*]

SAM: [*over-sweetly*] Champagne?

MIKE: Not for me . . . I'm on duty.

JO: You're always on bloody duty.

RUTH: Not for much longer.

SAM: What's this? Family's losing its hero?

MIKE: I'm being put out to grass. New directive. Fifty-five and you're off the boat.

RUTH: Six months from now and we can do what we like.

MIKE: Aye.

SAM: Oh, I'm sure you'll find some way of hanging on. Knowing you, you'll end up being the winch-man.

MIKE: And stand there watching the boat going out? No way . . .

LUKE: Anyhow, Bill's the winch-man.

MIKE: Aye . . . that job's spoken for.

SAM: Bill? He must be older than Jonah by now . . .

> [MIKE *looks at him.*]

RUTH: Well . . . cheers! Welcome home, Sam.

ALL: [*except* MIKE] Cheers!

SAM: *Salute!*

> [*Everyone, except* MIKE, *responds and takes a sip of their champagne.*]

MIKE: I should get back to the boathouse. With the weather like this . . .

RUTH: But Sam's only just got here.

MIKE: It's my job to check the boat. It's what I'm paid for. 'Cos I'm not a bloody hero. I just happen to do something that matters.

> [MIKE *leaves.*]

RUTH: God help us. The closer he gets to retiring, the less we see of him. He's finding it hard.

LUKE: Aye . . . it can't be easy for him . . .

JO: It's not easy for any of us.

LUKE: He's given everything to that boat.

HELEN: He's really gonna miss it . . .

JO: Well, I'm not.

RUTH: Jo . . . we've just six months to get through, then who knows –

SAM: Look . . . I'm really bushed. Jet lag and all that. I think I'd better crash out.

RUTH: . . . Fine. I've made up the bed in your old room.

SAM: Thanks, Mum.

> [*He picks up his bags and makes to go.*]

RUTH: Sam . . .

> [SAM *stops and looks at her.*]

It's good to have you home . . .

SAM: . . . Yeah. Good to be here . . .

> [*Pause.* SAM *turns to* LUKE, JO *and* HELEN.]

I'll . . . er . . . see you tomorrow, then.

> [*Pause.*]

RUTH: Sweet dreams, Sam.

> [SAM *leaves.*]

LUKE: Well . . . I'd better go and help Dad. You know what he's like . . .

JO: . . . we do . . .

HELEN: You have to?

LUKE: I'm sorry . . . but with the weather like this . . .

RUTH: [*to* HELEN]: I wouldn't fight it, love. It's not the weather, it's the boat. And the boat always wins.

LUKE: Come on . . . I'll walk you to the bus stop on the way . . .

> [LUKE *pulls on his coat.* HELEN *reluctantly gets up.*]

RUTH: Thank you for coming, Helen. Say hello to your mam.

HELEN: I will. And thank you for the . . . sandwiches . . .

LUKE: See you later.

> [LUKE *and* HELEN *leave. Pause.* JO *gets up abruptly.*]

JO: So much for taking the night off work. That's twenty quid down the drain.

RUTH: Is that all you can think of? Sam's home!

JO: Is he?

> [*She leaves to go upstairs.* RUTH *begins to clear up.* JO's *music begins to thump from upstairs.* RUTH

*stops and picks up her glass of champagne. She goes
to the window and looks out.*]

[*The lights fade to black.*]

Scene Two

Luke's workshop. Wednesday morning.

*Lights up. In the workshop there is a ladder leading
up to a small hatch in the ceiling. There may or may
not be benches but there are chairs that* LUKE *has been
working on.* LUKE *is sanding a chair and listening to the
local radio station on a small radio. SFX: 'Blow My
Whistle Baby' by DJ Alligator loudly through the house
system during the scene change and then only coming
out of* LUKE'*s radio as the lights come up.*

DJ: And that was 'Blow My Whistle Baby' by DJ Alligator, specially for Andrea Slatter from Kirkleatham.
Happy 18th, Andrea. Enjoy! And now for a bit of
local weather. You can expect it to be cold and wet
with cloudy skies and even some fog later on. Tem-
perature's about average for October, maximum
four degrees Celsius, thirty-nine degrees Fahrenheit.
Where's global warming when you need it?

[*SFX: intro to 'YMCA' by the Village People, over
which the DJ speaks.*]

This is Sall the Gal here with you for the next two
hours. Let's give it a go with one you all know. It's
a blast from the past . . . it's 'YMCA'!

[LUKE *bops around to the song, still sanding, but
getting increasingly carried away.* SAM *enters.* LUKE
*doesn't see him, lost in his silly dance. Then as he
spins round he sees him and stops, embarrassed.
He goes over to the radio and turns it off.*]

SAM: You should give this up and become a strip-o-gram.

LUKE: Shut it.

SAM: You could arrive in your butch lifeboat gear and peel it all off to reveal an orange pouch with a little slot for donations. [*looks around*] I can't believe it . . . my little brother getting this together. When did the polar bears move out?

LUKE: I'm gonna get a paraffin stove . . . over there . . . that should do the trick.

SAM: You renting it or what?

LUKE: At the moment . . . but they want to sell it and they've said they'll wait till I've enough for a deposit.

SAM: You've lucked out, big time . . .

LUKE: Yeah . . . and upstairs it's even better. Hard to get to right now . . . have to squeeze up that ladder . . . but it's just one big space and beams everywhere. Storage heaven!

SAM: Can you see the sea from up there?

LUKE: Only if you knocked a hole in the wall.

SAM: Go for it . . . it's called a window.

LUKE: I don't need a window . . .

SAM: Then maybe you could make some real stairs and move a few things up there . . . you know, a couple of chairs, an old sofa, a fridge, a TV. Maybe even a bed . . .

LUKE: And *live* here?

SAM: You going to live at home forever? You know people'd *kill* for a space like this in New York.

LUKE: They should move to Teesmouth, then. [*Pause.*] Look . . . I should be getting on . . . there's tons to do. I've borrowed a van to bring the lathes over tonight so I've got to sort out where they're going.

SAM: D'you want a hand?

LUKE: No. No. I'm fine. You must be knackered.

SAM: Oh, come on. I don't mind getting my hands dirty . . .

> [*He picks up a mop and begins to clean the floor.*]

LUKE: Cheers . . .

> [*He begins to sweep another part of the floor.*]

Sounds like it's going good over there.

SAM: Yeah. Good fun. Feel I'm driving in the fast lane with a blindfold on. Never short on adrenaline.

LUKE: Must be weird being home.

SAM: Yeah. Like walking though a photo album. 'Cept everyone's bigger than you remember.

LUKE: And they don't talk funny . . .

> [SAM *looks at him.*]

You can drop the accent while you're here . . .

SAM: But this is who I am now. I've run too far from this place to pretend nothing's changed.

> [*A beat.*]

I meant what I said, you know . . . this would be an awesome place to live.

LUKE: I can't believe I hadn't thought of it meself. But you're right . . . after all this time a place of my own . . .

SAM: And it's big enough for two . . .

> [LUKE *looks at him.*]

Don't you wanna wake up with her every morning?

LUKE: We've never talked about it.

SAM: Do you love her?

LUKE: Yeah. Who wouldn't?

SAM: And then you've got it all. Work, a place to live, apple of your father's eye, a beautiful girl . . .

LUKE: . . . who hasn't said 'yes' . . .

SAM: Knowing your luck, she will. You always fall on your feet. [*Pause.*] So what does she do, huh?

LUKE: She works at the wildlife sanctuary. Fighting pollution and saving rare birds and that.

SAM: Well . . . short men who make wobbly chairs are an endangered species.

LUKE: She's got this campaign together to try and stop the chemical plant pumping stuff into the river. She never stops reading about it. She really cares.

SAM: Wow . . . that's amazing . . .

LUKE [*looks worried*] What if she says 'no'?

SAM: Why would she do that?

LUKE: I just don't know what she sees in me.

SAM: [*thinks*] No. I can't think of anything, either.

LUKE: Oh, sod off . . .

> [*They get back to work.* SAM *bends down to pick at something stuck on the floor.* LUKE's *cleaning has taken him out of sight.* HELEN *enters. She sees the tempting bottom, sneaks up behind it, and pinches it.*]

SAM: Ow!

> [*He turns round, startled.* HELEN *is hugely embarrassed.*]

HELEN: I'm sorry . . . I thought you were . . . I'm so sorry.

SAM: Don't worry about it. Nicest thing that's happened to me since I got back.

> [*They look at each other, grinning, slightly lost in each other.* LUKE *returns and watches them for a moment.*]

LUKE: Hello.

HELEN: Hello. I was just passing and I thought I'd say . . . hello.

LUKE: Right.

> [*Pause.*]

SAM: [*to* LUKE] Look, I should be getting back. Check the mails and all that. I'll see you later.

LUKE: Yeah. Thanks for helping.

SAM: You're welcome.

> [*He turns to* HELEN, *smiling.*]

See you around.

> [*He leaves, jokingly protecting his bottom. Pause.*]

LUKE: So you came to say hello.

HELEN: Yes. [*A beat.*] 'Cos I missed you last night. And I fancied a hug on my way to work.

LUKE: Then why are we standing here like two daft buggers?

> [*They both relax, move to each other and hug.*]

HELEN: It's looking nice in here. Really coming on.

LUKE: Yeah . . . though I found some woodworm in the beams. I'll have to get that treated.

HELEN: Aw . . . I like woodworm. You know the larvae live in the wood for up to five years but when they emerge as adult beetles they've only got two or three weeks to lay their eggs before they die. Seems a bit sad somehow.

LUKE: Not half as sad as the roof falling in.

HELEN: I know. It's just they don't mean any harm. They're just baby beetles eating away.

LUKE: Great. Now I feel like Herod.

HELEN: [*laughs*] Don't worry . . . I won't report you to the RSPCA.

LUKE: Now before you rush off to save the world, I've got a question for you. [*Pause as he braces himself.*] How would you feel about waking up every morning with the best view of the sea in Teesmouth?

HELEN: Sorry?

LUKE: How would you feel about breakfast in bed while watching the oyster-catchers on the beach?

HELEN: What you on about?

LUKE: Upstairs is the perfect flat. It's just four walls and a roof right now but when I've finished it it's gonna be my home.

HELEN: You're going to *live* here?

LUKE: Aye. I've decided. [*A beat.*] But it won't be finished till you're in it . . .

HELEN: You and me . . . living together? *Here* . . .

LUKE: Yeah! And in the corner, just by the bed, there's going to be some shelves, just for nice things, ornaments and that . . .

> [*He brings out something wrapped in a dirty cloth. He gives it to* HELEN.]

HELEN: What is it?

LUKE: It's the last time I carve anything out of oak, that's what it is . . .

HELEN: You *made* it?

LUKE: I haven't quite finished it yet . . . I was going to varnish it . . . but . . .

> [HELEN *gingerly unwraps it. It is a beautiful wood carving of a heron.*]

HELEN: Oh Luke . . . it's lovely . . .

LUKE: Well, you're always going on about herons so I thought I'd make you one that doesn't fly away.

HELEN: No one's ever given me anything this beautiful . . . I didn't know you did carving.

LUKE: Nor did I. But I enjoyed it. I might do some more . . . but in pine.

HELEN: You should. It's beautiful. It really is.

LUKE: So would you like to see where it might go then? It's a right mess up there now and I'll need to put a window in but –

HELEN: Luke, can we just take it easy for a while . . . ?

LUKE: Sure . . . whatever you like . . . it'll be a while before it's ready anyhow so there's no rush . . .

> [*Long pause.*]

HELEN: Look, I should go . . . I've still got loads of research to do for the meeting tomorrow.

LUKE: Right. Well, good luck with it.

HELEN: I'll need it. They're as unpleasant as the stuff they pump into the sea.

LUKE: Give 'em hell.

> [*A beat.* HELEN *indicates the carved heron.*]

HELEN: Can I leave this here for a while?

LUKE: It can stay as long as you like . . .

        [HELEN *smiles and kisses him.* LUKE *takes the heron.*
        HELEN *makes to go.*]

        Helen . . . are you . . . proud of me . . . on the boat,
        I mean?

        [HELEN *is thrown.*]

        I mean . . . you don't wish I was doing something
        else . . . like Sam or something . . .

HELEN: You . . . behind a desk . . . wouldn't be you, would
        it . . . ?

        [*She leaves.* LUKE *watches her go and looks at the
        heron. He turns the radio back on. SFX: 'Lying in
        the Sun' by the Stereophonics, which continues
        during the scene change.*]

                        Scene Three

        Wednesday. Early evening

        MIKE *is revealed in a pool of light. He is addressing the
        audience as if they were a group of new recruits.*

MIKE: So I'm glad you want to be lifeboat-men and I'm
        pleased to see you all here this evening. I'd like
        to thank the crew and the friends of the RNLI
        for putting on such a cracking presentation. But
        before you go, ask yourselves why you came here
        . . . Like boats? The sea? Saving lives? You spend
        months training, every weekend out there, learn-
        ing what it's all about. Drills, spills, cleaning the
        boat, studying charts and the latest computer sys-
        tems. But it's not about that. Never has been. So
        before you sign up, I'll tell you what it's about and
        then you can decide if you *really* want to be here or
        not. I'll tell you now.

[*He looks straight ahead, his eyes moving slowly across the audience. It becomes a very, very long pause. A minute. But his concentration never slips. Then finally he speaks again.*]

That's what it's about. Waiting. Being there. And it doesn't matter if it's ten men on a trawler in a force eight or a dog trapped by the tide. You never know when it's gonna happen. All you can do is wait till it does. I'm the coxswain and the mechanic. I can never be more than two miles from the boat unless I put the second coxswain on duty. But I don't like doing that. I want to be there. That's what it's about. That's the sacrifice. Going out there's the easy bit. It's being there that's hard.

[*The pool of light fades to black.*]

Scene Four

Wednesday night. The kitchen.

SFX: during the scene change we hear a computer modem connecting to the internet.

SAM *is working on his laptop at the kitchen table. He is on-line.* JO *is sitting at the other end of the table with a couple of large books open. She's flicking through them and then scribbling on a piece of paper.* RUTH *is reading a cookery book. There is a large envelope on the table beside her.*

JO: Bloody hell. Did you know that the dinosaurs died out 'cos they were constipated?

SAM: They died out because an asteroid hit the planet, causing cataclysmic climate change.

JO: Right. It was the climate change that killed off their usual food source and what they were left with made them constipated. Can you imagine it? All them brontosauruses straining away for weeks. All them pterodactyls farting their way through the air. Must have been the world's first jet propulsion.

SAM: Shouldn't you be at the pub?

JO: They've given me shift to the new girl. The one that got a look in 'cos I took last night off.

RUTH: Maybe she's polite to the customers.

JO: It's not that. She's got a cleavage like the Grand bloody Canyon. I swear, when the customers order their drinks . . . it echoes.

SAM: Well I'm sorry if you've lost some money because of me. But right now I'm trying to work.

JO: So am I.

SAM: You? Work? This is the first time I've ever seen you read a book.

JO: Yeah. Well. Miss Cleavage can't think and talk at the same time so they've put me in charge of the pub quiz. I've got to come up with fifty questions for Saturday lunch-time.

SAM: Then get on with it. Quietly. Or *you'll* become extinct.

JO: I just thought you'd be interested . . .

[*Pause as they both get back to work.* SAM *pores over his emails.*]

SAM: Yes!

RUTH: What is it?

SAM: We're up and running! Well . . . we will be soon . . .

JO: I thought the dot-com bubble had burst . . .

SAM: It has . . . but there's still a killing to be made if the idea's good enough. And this one's amazing.

JO: Even if you say it yourself.

SAM: I've been involved in enough non-starters to know. Which is why I've set up on my own. It's the only way forward.

RUTH: How d'you manage that?

SAM: My business partner, Casey, his dad plays golf, and his golfing partner is loaded and he's just given us the thumbs up on some seed funding . . .

JO: So you're Mr New York 'cos your mate's dad plays golf with some rich bastard . . .

SAM: He believes in me. That's what it's all about. We're not talking reality here. We're talking faith.

JO: So what are you selling now? Bibles?

SAM: No. It's a kind of conceptual thing . . . you wouldn't understand it.

JO: Oh, that's right. I forgot. I still live in Teesmouth so I must be very stupid.

RUTH: Come on, Sam . . . unless it's a secret . . .

SAM: [*to* JO] OK. OK. Have you ever had a personal problem of any kind?

JO: [*warily*] Maybe . . .

SAM: Oh, come on . . . *everyone* has. At some time in our lives something goes wrong and pow! We need help. Whether it's how to deal with exam stress, build self-esteem, survive Christmas with the in-laws, whatever. And that's what's so great about this website . . . it deals with the downside of the human condition. And that's a constant.

JO: And don't tell me . . . you've got all the answers . . .

SAM: Sure. Well, I *personally* haven't. But the aim of the site is to link up those who have the problems with those who can help.

RUTH: An on-line agony aunt . . .

SAM: It's much bigger than that! You log on to the site
from wherever you are, no travelling, no embarrass-
ment, and you're given three options. Choose
number one and you get through to . . . well . . . yes,
an agony aunt. You describe your problem and he
or she immediately responds. But unlike a magazine
you can reply, asking more, clarifying what your
problem is . . .

RUTH: Marge Proops goes digital.

SAM: Chose number two and a list comes up of all the
classic problems – my wife's just run off with
another guy, my father doesn't understand me, I'm
fifty on Friday – and you click on the appropriate
one and the site immediately puts you in touch with
people who have the same problem. Then you meet
them in a chat-room on the site and share your
experiences. Virtual co-counselling.

JO: Can't people just go to pubs?

SAM: Click on option three and you're given a list of types
of therapy – psychoanalysis, cognitive behavioural
therapy, gestalt therapy, transactional analysis,
existential therapy – whatever you want. You
simply choose one and then make an appointment
with the relevant therapist. The sessions take place
in a private chat-room at the appointed hour, either
as a one-off or as a regular thing. And there you go
. . . the world's a happier place and I'm a richer man.

JO: This makes you money?

SAM: Of course. The golfing partner'll subsidise us for a
while but once it's taken off we'll be raking it in.
There's a sliding scale of payment – from a small-
ish fee for the agony aunt to a rather large fee for

the one-to-one professional therapy. And the company, that's me, takes a cut of everything!

JO: So . . . you're looking for people who are unhappy and charging them for it.

[SAM *begins to write out a cheque.*]

SAM: [*to* JO] Seeing as you're so understanding of what your big brother does, I think you should have this.

[*He gives her the cheque then starts to pack up his laptop.*]

JO: What's this? It's not even my birthday.

SAM: I think it's time you stopped dreaming about it and booked yourself some flights.

JO: Two thousand dollars!

SAM: Enough for the flight and to keep you safe for a couple of weeks till you find your feet.

JO: Sam . . . I don't know what to say . . .

SAM: You? Speechless? It's worth every cent.

JO: I can't believe it!

SAM: I'll see you later.

[*He kisses her on the top of her head.*]

Ciao!

[*He leaves.*]

JO: I can go. This means I can actually go! I can book the flight!

RUTH: Jo . . . does it have to be Thailand?

JO: What's wrong with Thailand?

RUTH: Last year Lisa, you know, Lucy's daughter, spent the summer in France in huge greenhouses planting chrysanthemums.

JO: I want to go scuba-diving. I want somewhere that's different, *really* different, somewhere I'll never forget. Not bloody chrysanthemums.

RUTH: But Thailand. It's not safe.

JO: Mam! People get stabbed in Teesmouth! What am I meant to do? Stay in me room forever?

RUTH: You do that already.

JO: Maybe when Dad retires you could both come out and we'll meet up in Bali.

RUTH: Can you imagine your father in Bali? Paddling in the waves? 'Bout as likely as Middlesbrough winning the league. Anyway, he doesn't retire for another six months yet . . . you'll be back by then.

JO: Depends what happens, who I meet . . .

RUTH: You're not making this easy . . .

JO: Who for?

RUTH: Me! Your father! What d'you think he's gonna say when he hears you've got the money?

JO: I don't care. And at least I'm brave enough to tell him what my plans are.

RUTH: That's enough.

JO: No it isn't. I've spent years dreaming about me trip and Sam's made it happen. Now it's time you made *your* plans happen.

RUTH: Jo . . . you don't know what you're saying.

JO: How long have you been planning and saving behind Dad's back? Why don't you just tell him?

RUTH: It's not the right time, that's all.

JO: It'll *never* be the right time. You've just got to tell him. It's a good plan. He'll jump at it!

RUTH: You think so?

JO: You'll never know unless you tell him.

[*Pause.*]

RUTH: Maybe you're right. You know I heard from the estate agent yesterday.

JO: Why didn't you tell me?

RUTH: 'Cos I knew you'd give me a hard time about telling your father . . .

JO: If I don't give you a hard time you'll never get to Cornwall. [*A beat.*] So come on, what did the estate agent say?

RUTH: He thinks he's found the perfect place.

JO: At last!

[RUTH *opens the large envelope, takes out the details, and gives them to* JO.]

RUTH: It's in a little village on the coast. He reckons it needs a lot of work but it's big enough and within my price range.

JO: It's pink with white shutters!

RUTH: I shouldn't think your father would leave it pink for long. But don't you think it's perfect?

JO: Yes! You have to go for it *now* . . . before someone else gets it.

RUTH: I know. The estate agent says I should put an offer in by the end of the week.

JO: So now's the time to tell Dad. You can't leave it any longer.

RUTH: You're right. I'll tell him tonight.

JO: Nice one! But if I'm still in Thailand when it happens, don't forget to tell me your new address or I won't be able to send you postcards.

RUTH: You'd better be back by then, my girl.

JO: Oh, I see. It's only Sam who can go away for years . . .

[MIKE *enters, singing.* RUTH *hides the envelope.*]

MIKE: 'As I was a-walking down Paradise Street
Singing! Whey hey blow the man down
A handsome flash packet I chanced for to meet
Hoy! Gimme some time to blow the man down.'

[*He takes* RUTH *in his arms and dances with her as
he sings, twirling her around.* RUTH *is surprised but
enjoys it.* JO *watches, amazed.*]

'She was bowling along with the wind blowing free
Singing! Whey hey blow the man down
She threwed up her courses and hoved to to me!
Hoy! Gimme some time to blow the man down.'

[RUTH *breaks free, laughing.*]

RUTH: What's got into you, then?

MIKE: Can't a man be happy without some reason?

RUTH: Not that *I've* ever known. So it's either a woman, a
boat or a pint. And by the looks of it, it's the last one.

MIKE: Met the new recruits. Usual bunch of glory-seekers.
Put most of 'em off, thank God. Then had to go to
choir practice. So I put the second coxswain on duty.
Then I went out with the boys. To the Anchor!

JO: Your one night off and you went to the pub?

MIKE: Aye. And they've got a new barmaid there. Very
impressive. We had a very nice chat.

JO: Expert in navigation, is she?

[*She leaves abruptly.*]

MIKE: What's the matter with her?

RUTH: Being here.

MIKE: She's not still going on about Thailand is she?

RUTH: Stubborn as a mule, that one.

MIKE: No daughter of mine is going to some fly-by-night unregistered diving school somewhere in bloody Thailand. I've pulled enough divers out of the sea to know what I'm talking about.

RUTH: She won't listen.

MIKE: She's a bloody child and this travelling business is proving it!

RUTH: She's got a nose for danger, that girl. Can't think why.

MIKE: So it's *my* bloody fault, is it?

RUTH: She's gonna do it whether we want her to or not.

MIKE: Wish I'd stayed in the pub!

RUTH: Mike, this isn't going to go away. We have to talk about it. Kids leave. It's what they do.

MIKE: Luke isn't.

RUTH: Aye. And we should be grateful for that. But Jo's like Sam –

MIKE: No one in this family's like Sam! We do things for people. We help people. Like my father died out there helping people! All he's interested in is helping himself and lining his pockets!

RUTH: You don't even *know* what he does!

MIKE: I don't have to! He's a taker, that one. Always has been.

RUTH: He's your son!

MIKE: Aye. And I bloody wish he wasn't!

[*He storms out of the house.*]

[*Blackout.*]

Scene Five

Thursday morning

SFX: during the scene change we hear 'Lying in the Sun' by the Stereophonics.

HELEN *is revealed in a pool of light. She is addressing the audience as if they were the management of the local chemical plant. She is holding some prompt cards and is very nervous.*

HELEN: And finally we want to show you another way in which your manufacturing methods are endangering our fragile eco-system around Teesside. I'm sure you're already aware of the damaging effects of dimorphism in both fish and shellfish. This process is irreversible, causing the fish, along with periwinkles, mussels, dog whelks and cockles, to become permanently infertile. The overall stock is depleted and so everything in the food chain suffers, including birds. Even humans eating the shellfish may be affected. We've come here to ask that your procedures for cleaning the reaction vessels are changed and that the chemicals are no longer rinsed directly into the estuary without first being treated.

Look . . . what I'm trying to say is, in today's society we all enjoy enormous freedom to do what we like. But while we make our choices we have to be responsible for the lives of those we share our planet with. And the lives within the sea are just as important as those on the land. We depend on the life of the sea and any compromising of that life will impoverish our own lives and those of every generation yet to come. We have to listen to our planet. We have to listen to ourselves. Or else we will lose the most important habitat of all . . . our home.

[*There is a long, uneasy pause.*]

Do you have any questions?

[*SFX: the sea. Long pause as she looks anxiously around. The SFX continue during the scene change.*]

[*The pool of light fades to black.*]

Scene Six

The kitchen. Thursday lunch-time.

Lights up on HELEN *and* LUKE.

LUKE: How did it go?

HELEN: Bloody awful. They just sat there. Didn't give a shit.

LUKE: Well, it's a start . . .

HELEN: Oh Luke, I felt such a fool. Standing there trying to make a load of smug bastards care.

LUKE: Come on, let's go down the pub and talk about it.

HELEN: No. Your mam's made an effort. I'll be fine.

LUKE: You sure?

HELEN: I'll just put me smile on.

[*The lights come up on* RUTH, MIKE, SAM *and* JO *sitting at the table.* RUTH *is serving out the lunch.* HELEN *and* LUKE *take their places at the table. As they talk they eat – with chopsticks.*]

RUTH: How was it, love?

SAM: D'ya knock 'em dead?

HELEN: I think we can safely say they were dead. This looks lovely.

RUTH: Oh, it's nothing. I'm just sorry your mam couldn't come.

HELEN: She's a bit behind with her costume for tomorrow.

JO: Who's she going as?

HELEN: Joan of Arc.

MIKE: Before or after she was burned at the stake . . . ?

> [*He laughs.*]

HELEN: [*to* SAM] So tell us about New York . . .

SAM: It's just, like, a crazy place. Can't believe your eyes half the time. Like last week I saw this guy, sitting on the sidewalk, filthy he was, as down and out as you get, skin blistered by the sun, stinking like a frightened skunk, and he's holding out a cup, asking for money. And on the side of the cup it says, 'I Love New York'. [*A beat.*] And then the next day there's this woman walking round Times Square, completely naked, protesting about –

MIKE: Are these good stories to be telling your sister?

SAM: They're not stories. They're real. It's what you see if you go more than two miles from the boathouse.

MIKE: If it wasn't for the two mile rule there'd be lives lost.

SAM: And others lived . . .

> [*Awkward pause.*]

LUKE: So what *is* this, Mam?

RUTH: Papaya and chilli noodles with tofu marinated in lime and sesame oil.

> [*They all look at her and then drop their chopsticks. A beat. Suddenly a maroon goes off.* MIKE *and* LUKE *immediately get up and without even looking at anyone else they run out of the house.* HELEN *rushes after them as far as the door.*]

HELEN: [*calls out*] Look after yourself, Luke!

[*Pause. She then turns back to the table, embarrassed.*]

I guess you don't do that any more.

RUTH: I did for the first year or two. But they don't hear, anyway. [*Pause.*] Come on. Let's eat.

[HELEN *slowly sits down at the table but can't face the food.*]

SAM: Look, it can't be that bad. There's a little wind but it's not as if there's a hurricane or something. [*Pause. to* RUTH] They'll be all right, won't they?

[RUTH *nods.* SAM *gets up to go.*]

RUTH: Where you going?

SAM: I've got that presentation tomorrow . . . I need to work on it . . .

[*He leaves, taking his plate with him. The three women sit in silence for a while.*]

HELEN: Why don't you have a home radio here? When Dad was alive we all sat round and listened to them talking to the coastguards.

RUTH: We used to. Then a couple of years ago I heard Mike tell the coastguards that one of the crew had been washed overboard. It was two hours before I knew it wasn't Luke. I'd rather not know till they're back.

[*A beat.* HELEN *breaks away from the table.*]

HELEN: How do you manage? If anything happened to Luke –

JO: Oh, he'll be back. You know sometimes I see him looking out to sea as if he's *wishing* something would go wrong. Just so he can go and be a hero.

RUTH: Now, Jo . . .

JO: It's true. I've even heard Dad say that some of the young uns are as bad as wreckers.

RUTH: Aye. And they're the ones that never make it. Luke's not like that. He's keen, but that don't make him a wrecker.

[JO *leaves*.]

HELEN: I just don't know why they do it.

[*A beat.*]

RUTH: Where did you and Luke have your first kiss?

HELEN: Sorry?

RUTH: I assume you have kissed by now . . .

HELEN: Er . . . on the beach.

RUTH: Of course you did. It's where Mike proposed to me. It's where people go when they're lonely, or when they're celebrating, or when they've just had a row and need to calm down. It's the sea. It fills in the gaps.

HELEN: Right now it feels like it *makes* the gaps.

RUTH: Aye. Just being on the beach isn't enough for some. They need to be *on* the sea, sometimes even *in* the bloody thing. Then they're out of reach . . .

[JO *returns*.]

We should sort our costumes out for Friday.

HELEN: I can't think about that now.

JO: It helps to think about something else.

RUTH: Aye. And after all, we have to keep fund-raising.

HELEN: Why? So they can keep going out there?

RUTH: Fun, isn't it . . . ?

[*The lights fade to black.* RUTH *begins her song during the scene change.*]

Scene Seven

The kitchen. Late Thursday night.

Lights up on RUTH. *She is sitting sewing an old shirt. As she sews she is quietly singing to herself.*

RUTH: 'As I was a-walking down Paradise Street
Singing! Whey hey blow the man down
A handsome flash packet I chanced for to meet
Hoy! Gimme some time to blow the man down.

She was bowling along with the wind blowing free
Singing! Whey hey blow the man down . . .'

> [*She stops and looks around. Then she puts the material to one side, gets up and looks out of the window. Nothing. After a while she goes back and resumes her sewing. At last the door opens and* MIKE *walks in. He is exhausted.* RUTH *watches him, alarmed, unable to speak. He slowly moves across the room, pulls out a chair at the table and slumps down.* RUTH, *her alarm growing to fear, stares at him.*]

Mike . . . look at me!

> [MIKE *looks up, drained.*]

Where is he?

MIKE: Who?

RUTH: Luke! Where's Luke!

MIKE: He went off to see Helen. He'll be back soon.

RUTH: You might have bloody said!

> [MIKE *looks away, too exhausted to respond.*]

What was it?

MIKE: A yacht. Family day out. Father hadn't a bloody clue. Too much sail. Capsized. Fished out the mother and father. Cold. In shock. Two boys trapped under-

neath. In an air pocket. Thank God. Took us half
an hour to get 'em out. [*Pause.*] Only found the girl
when another boat with a diver arrived. Her hair
had got trapped in a door as it snapped shut when
the boat went over. Never stood a chance. [*Pause.*]
She was seven.

> [*He cries.* RUTH *goes to him and holds him.* MIKE *responds and they hold each other for a long time.*]
>
> [*The lights slowly fade to black.*]

Scene Eight

Friday morning.

SFX: during the scene change we hear a stormy sea.

SAM *is revealed in a pool of light. He is addressing the
audience as if they were the Newcastle Chamber of
Commerce. He speaks in a Geordie accent.*

SAM: So that's where I am and that's where I'm going.
I could have made this pretty. I could have brought
you some clever images thrown up on a screen
generated by Silicon Valley's finest, and tweaked to
perfection by my own team. But I haven't. I've just
brought me. And you know why? Because I'm not
interested in selling. If you want to buy into this it's
gotta be for one reason and one reason alone. You
trust me. Doubt me and we walk away. 'Cos this isn't
about images. It's not even about facts and figures.
We all know how we can make those add up to mean
anything. No. This is only about vision.

Right now it's Virtual Therapy. As I've said, we've
hit the market hard and it's responding. But that's
just the beginning. Let's make this personal. I have
more ideas than Hitchcock had nightmares. I *bleed*

ideas. Let me tell you, gentlemen, we're already rich. Rich in inspiration.

Now there are people who'd stand here and try to persuade you to invest. I know that. People who are small trying to be big. For God's sake, people who are only funded because their friend's father happens to play golf with some rich bloke. But that's not me. I'm here to ask you to join us in riding the fastest wave that's come along since Noah started surfing, and if you want to come on board, great. If you don't, then sit back, read about where we're going and weep. It's gonna be a good ride. Believe me. 'Cos if it wasn't, I wouldn't be here today.

So be simple. Be clear. Believe a little and we all win. Be cynical and only you lose. That's all you need to know. Thank you for your time.

[*The pool of light fades to black.*]

Scene Nine

The kitchen. Friday. Late afternoon.

We hear LUKE, JO, MIKE, SAM *and* HELEN *singing 'Happy Birthday' offstage.*

The remains of a dodgy-looking cake are sitting on the table, surrounded by plates of unfinished slices. MIKE *and* RUTH *are sitting at the table.* MIKE *is pouring them both a couple of beers.*

RUTH: Bless her . . . can't believe Jo made me a cake.

MIKE: That isn't a cake, it's a health hazard.

RUTH: It's the effort that counts.

MIKE: Aye. The effort of eating it.

RUTH: And thank you for the barbecue . . . now I can cook outside in the summer.

MIKE: It were Luke's idea. Nowt to do with me.

RUTH: Mike . . . it's me birthday . . . you can be nice if you like . . .

[MIKE *looks at her.*]

MIKE: Happy birthday, love.

[*They kiss.*]

We'd better get ready for the do. They'll be ready before us at this rate.

RUTH: I've got it all here, love.

[*She opens a large box. They talk as she unpacks it, pulling out straw hats, shirts and braces, baggy trousers, etc.*]

MIKE: What's this? We always go as pirates. Why aren't we going as pirates? Everyone knows we go as pirates!

RUTH: We lost the parrot.

MIKE: So?

RUTH: This year we're going as farmers.

MIKE: Farmers?

RUTH: Old-fashioned Cornish farmers. So we'll be on cider all night.

MIKE: Bloody hell . . . can't believe we're going as land-lubbers.

RUTH: Well, we are.

[*She plonks a big straw hat on his head to emphasise the point. They begin to get dressed and continue throughout their conversation.*]

Kids are getting on great, aren't they?

MIKE: Aye.

RUTH: I've got a good feeling about tonight.

MIKE: Should be a good do.

RUTH: How long has it been since I had the whole family together for me birthday?

MIKE: If I remember right it were a Pirates and Smugglers evening. Sam got pissed and threw up in a barrel.

[RUTH *laughs.*]

RUTH: That's right! And one of the crew was hiding in it. He was planning to jump out as a surprise but it was *him* who got the surprise!

MIKE: Poor lad stank of rum and carrots for the rest of the night!

[RUTH *laughs. Pause.*]

What I said about Sam the other night . . .

RUTH: You were drunk. I never heard it.

MIKE: I don't like what he does but –

RUTH: So let's leave it.

[*She busies herself with the costumes, staying breezy and light.*]

D'you know, he gave Jo a huge cheque the other day.

MIKE: What? Money? Our Jo?

RUTH: Towards her trip to Thailand.

MIKE: What the hell did he do that for?

RUTH: He wanted to help.

MIKE: Help her get herself killed in some bloody diving school! [*A beat.*] Her and her big ideas.

RUTH: There's nowt wrong with big ideas. I've been having some of me own.

MIKE: Will you help me with these braces?

RUTH: It's a sort of plan.

MIKE: A plan?

RUTH: Well, you know in six months' time, when you retire –

MIKE: Aye, and although it's a little way off, as all the kids are here, I thought I'd make a little speech tonight. You don't mind, do you? Nothing fancy. I'd just say, oh hell, these damned braces . . . never had this problem when I was a pirate . . .

[RUTH *sorts his braces out.*]

I'll say, well, you know, thanks for all the donations and that. And then I'll say, 'Now you haven't seen the back of me yet. As you all know, Bill Partridge is retiring in a few months, and the board have asked me, and I've said I'd be honoured, so you're looking at your new winch-man.'

[RUTH *is stunned.* MIKE *turns to her.*]

You know, I never thought I could stand being the winch-man, but ever since Sam mentioned it, it's been ticking over in me mind. It's an important job, you know. Can't have a launch without a winch-man.

[*Just at that moment* JO, SAM, HELEN *and* LUKE *rush into the room in their fancy dress. They are dressed as versions of the Village People:* JO *is the Construction Worker,* SAM *is the Cowboy,* HELEN *is the Biker and* LUKE *is the Red Indian Chief, complete with lots of face and body make-up and a feather headdress.*]

JO/SAM/HELEN/LUKE: Da-da!

MIKE: Bloody hell!

JO: What d'ya think, Mam?

RUTH: I think . . . you look . . . very nice . . .

SAM: And there's more. We've prepared a little something to help with the fund-raising.

JO: And we want to show you before we go!

LUKE: Do we have to?

JO: Come on!

> [*They line up and begin to sing, complete with choreography, to the tune of 'YMCA' by the Village People.*]

HELEN: 1,2,3,4 –

JO/SAM/HELEN/LUKE:

> Young man – you're the king of the seas
> I said young man – sailing out from the Tees
> I said young man – if your rigging should freeze
> We will be there in a jiffy.
>
> Bap bap bap bap bap
>
> For altogether we're the RNLI
> In any weather we're the RNLI
> We've a jolly nice boat
> You can keep it afloat
> If you give us a donation.
>
> Bap bap bap bap bap
>
> For altogether we're the RNLI
> In any weather –

> [*A maroon goes off. A beat.* LUKE *and* MIKE *rush off, still in fancy dress.*]

JO: Bloody hell!

> [*Blackout.*]

End of Act One

ACT TWO

Scene One

Luke's workshop. Late Friday night.

SFX: the intro to 'YMCA' by the Village People.

The music stops as the lights come up. LUKE *enters, still in his Red Indian Chief costume but dripping wet, make-up running all down his face and body, looking thoroughly fed up. He is carrying the headdress.*

LUKE: [*throwing down the headdress*] Bloody hell . . . bloody hell!

      [HELEN *rushes in.*]

What the hell are you playing at? I came here for a bit of peace and quiet.

      [HELEN *laughs.*]

HELEN: I know. I was waiting at the house and I saw your dad. He said you'd come here so I wouldn't see you . . . so I ran straight over.

LUKE: I can't believe it. As if it wasn't bad enough arriving at this fishing boat looking like bloody 'Dances With Wolves'. The crew couldn't believe their eyes when they saw us. After we'd rescued them they just took the piss out of us all the way home. Then we get to the harbour and there's all the bloody press there. And we had to line up looking like this while they took photos of us. I've never felt such a tit.

HELEN: Well, I think you look very sexy.

LUKE: Thanks a bunch . . .

[*He starts to take off his wet gear.*]

HELEN: It's getting better all the time . . .

LUKE: If you've just come to take the piss . . .

HELEN: Course not. It's my job to rescue feathered creatures . . .

LUKE: I'm never going to live this down, am I?

HELEN: No. But you'll be glad to hear that after you rushed off we had a great time.

LUKE: You weren't even worried?

HELEN: No. When we got to the do someone had a radio there so we all listened in. We could hear you weren't in any danger. The coastguards were loving it.

LUKE: I know. They had a bloody field day. It's the last time I go to a fancy dress do, I'm telling you.

[*By now he's down to his underwear.* HELEN *slowly moves in on him, unzipping her jacket.*]

HELEN: [*very playful*] I reckon the only good thing about going out with a lifeboat-man is how fit it keeps 'em.

LUKE: Helen . . .

HELEN: We haven't christened this place yet, have we . . . ?

LUKE: Not now Helen . . . please . . .

HELEN: Come on . . . you look so sweet standing there next to all these big tools . . .

LUKE: Look. I'm knackered, all right. It may be a right laugh to you but it's hard bloody work out there and I'm fucking knackered!

[HELEN *turns away, embarrassed, hurt. She does up her jacket.* LUKE *hurriedly pulls some overalls on.*]

HELEN: Look. It's late. Why don't we just go back to mine
. . . We could watch a video, have a couple of beers,
calm down a bit . . .

LUKE: I'd love to . . . but we've got training first thing in
the morning and Dad's expecting me to check the
boat with him before the lads arrive.

HELEN: Please? You hardly ever come to my home, and
when you do we . . . and as soon as it's over you're
off. Back to the bloody boat.

LUKE: That's why I want you to move in with me. Here.
We could be together every night.

HELEN: Except when you're called out. And then I can't
sleep for worrying about you. And then you come
home God knows when and –

LUKE: I thought you understood . . .

HELEN: I do. Maybe it'd be easier if I didn't. I've seen it all
before.

LUKE: You want me to give it all up?

HELEN: Maybe you're just the wrong person.

LUKE: What?

HELEN: I was doing fine. Bit lonely, but fine. Then I fall for
you, and I love you and I want to be with you but
half of you's always with the boat. Well, I grew up
with that . . . and now it's bloody happening to me!

LUKE: But I love you!

HELEN: Then come back with me. Spend just one night away
from that boat. [*A beat.*] Luke. I want you to sleep
in my bed. I want us to wake up in the room I grew
up in. That's all I want.

LUKE: And you think I don't want that? You think I *want*
to be here? I *have* to . . . for the others . . .

HELEN: Do you?

LUKE: Listen . . . it's exciting out there. You feel like –

HELEN: The biggest bloody boy scout in the world. I know.
I watched me father come back again and again and
nothing made him happier. Not even me mam. And
that's what I don't want!

LUKE: No! It's not that! It's the sea, it's the sodding waves
. . . they scare the shit out of you . . . you don't know
what's going to happen . . . and the other men,
they're there for you, like no one else *can* be, and –

HELEN: So what am *I* doing then . . . ?

[*Pause.* LUKE *is thrown.*]

[*gently*] It's all right, Luke. You've already chosen.
You're married to the boat. It's just I don't want to
be your bit on the side.

[*She turns and leaves.*]

LUKE: I thought you were proud of me!

[*But she's gone.* LUKE *sags.*]

[*The lights fade to black.*]

Scene Two

Saturday lunch-time.

*SFX: during the scene change we hear 'Blow My Whistle
Baby' by DJ Alligator.*

JO *is revealed in a pool of light. She is addressing the audience as if they were the locals in the pub where she
works. She is speaking into a tinny microphone, reading out the questions for the pub quiz.*

JO: And here's the next one. Number 48. Was the in-
scription at the top of the crucifix INRI or RNLI?
[*Pause.*] And number 49. As we all know, Mark

Bolan was killed when his car crashed into a tree in Barnes Common. The year was 1977 but what kind of tree was it? [*Pause.*] And finally, number 50. And I want an exact answer here please. What caused the extinction of the dinosaurs? [*Pause.*] While Tina's collecting your papers I want to tell you I won't be working here any more. I've got me money now so I'll be off to Thailand in a few weeks. But I promise when I'm sipping cocktails on a beach in Koh Samui I'll be thinking of yous. I might even send you all a postcard. And I'd like to take this chance to say, Geoff, just hurry up and ask Mary out . . . we all know you fancy her. Jenny, good luck with the driving test . . . if you fail again you could always contact the *Guinness Book of Records.* And Frank, the new hair cut doesn't work. So from tomorrow I'll just be an ordinary customer and you're all welcome to buy me a farewell pint. Thank you.

[*The pool of light fades to black.*]

Scene Three

The kitchen. Saturday afternoon.

SFX: during the scene change we hear a computer modem connecting to the internet.

SAM *is at the table working on his laptop. He's on-line again. There is a glass of water near him.* JO *enters.*

JO: How's it going?

SAM: Fine. Just checking my mails.

JO: Any news on the website?

SAM: And to what do I owe this sudden burst of interest?

JO: You've been promoted . . . to favourite big brother of the year.

SAM: How very touching. Amazing what a cheque can do . . .

JO: Aye. I'm going to book me flight on Monday.

SAM: Good for you.

JO: Bye bye Teesmouth, bye bye pub, bye bye lifeboat.

SAM: You will look after yourself, won't you?

JO: Don't you bloody start.

[SAM *looks at the screen and reads.*]

Why does everyone think I'm going to end up a drug-smuggling lap-dancer with malaria?

SAM: [*still reading the screen*] Shit.

JO: What?

SAM: Nothing.

JO: Don't worry. P'raps we'll have a world recession and then you'll have *lots* of depressed people.

[SAM *is too busy reading to reply.*]

Charming. See you later.

[*She leaves.* SAM *continues reading then looks away. He disconnects from the internet. He looks round to check he's alone and then picks up the telephone and hurriedly dials.*]

SAM: Casey? It's Sam. What the hell's going on? . . . I've just got a mail from Clive . . . said he's pulling out . . . Why? . . . Swimming pools! Why's he suddenly so interested in swimming pools? . . . When did this happen? Why the hell didn't you tell me! . . . Because I could have called him! I could have talked to him! I could have . . . [*falters*] So now what do we do? . . . What? [*listens for a while, becoming increasingly pained, then bitter*] Well, how very cosy. Thanks for the support. And I hope you drown in one of the fucking things!

[*He slams the phone down and sinks into a chair. It wobbles. He puts his head in his hands.* RUTH *enters with some shopping bags.*]

RUTH: Afternoon, Sam. You had a good time last night. You know bartenders are meant to *sell* the booze, not drink it all.

[*She takes out a packet of pills from her shopping and puts them on the table.*]

Aspirin?

SAM: No . . . I'm fine . . . just tired . . .

RUTH: Look, I know you have to go tomorrow. I thought maybe we could go for a drink later. Catch up properly.

[SAM *quickly stands up and begins to pack up his laptop. Suddenly music starts from upstairs. SFX: 'Blow My Whistle Baby' by DJ Alligator.*]

Sam. Stop it.

SAM: What . . . ?

RUTH: Stop running away. I've hardly seen you since you got here. I don't even know how you are.

SAM: [*bitter*] Oh, that'll be good. Nothing like a good old heart to heart to put the world to rights. So tell me . . . what's your position on the morality of venture capitalists?

[RUTH *looks at him.* SAM *slumps back into his chair.*]

I'm sorry. Maybe I will have that aspirin after all. Got to be fit as a fiddle when I get back. Meetings, deadlines, closing the deal . . .

[*He takes the aspirin.*]

RUTH: And that makes you happy, does it?

SAM: Are you kidding? I've never *been* so happy!

RUTH: I'm glad to hear it.

SAM: I belong there. It's home.

[RUTH *looks away.*]

You get one idea right. Just one. Then they believe in you. And you sell it on as fast as you can and buy other ideas. You call them companies but that's all they really are . . . ideas. Then you sell *them* on, taking more and more risks, buying even *more* ideas till you've gone so far you can't go back. It scares the shit out of you . . . you don't know what's going to happen . . . but when you finally sell the big one, that's it. You're made for life.

RUTH: And if you don't?

SAM: You don't believe in me, do you?

RUTH: I've never liked gambling.

SAM: But it's the gamble I love. And right now I'm winning!

RUTH: Are you?

SAM: Yes! It might not last but I don't want to know what's going to happen! That's the point! Dad's always known. He's known every goddam day what he wants, what it's for, why he does it, what comes next. He's so fucking certain it doesn't leave room for anyone else!

[*He starts to go.*]

RUTH: Sam! Where are you going?

SAM: Where does *anyone* go round here?

[*He leaves. A beat.*]

RUTH: [*shouting upstairs*] Jo! Jo!

[*The music stops and* JO *appears.*]

JO: What?

RUTH: We're going out.

JO: Where?

RUTH: For some chips.

JO: I'm listening to my music.

RUTH: You're not listening to it, you're going deaf.

JO: I don't want to go out.

RUTH: We're going to get chips for dinner and meet the others.

JO: What?

RUTH: Go and tell your dad and Luke. Tell 'em we'll see 'em by the jetty.

JO: We're going to the *beach?*

RUTH: That's what it's there for.

JO: But it's raining!

RUTH: If they can manage to go out in all weathers on that bloody boat they can manage a bag of chips on the beach. Now go and tell 'em!

[JO *reluctantly goes out. The lights fade to black.*]

Scene Four

The beach. Saturday afternoon.

SFX: the sea.

During the scene the sound of the sea slowly builds and builds in volume and intensity. SAM *is by himself. He is throwing stones into the sea.* HELEN *arrives on the beach. She is on her way to the wildlife sanctuary carrying a plastic bottle of seawater. She sees* SAM *and stops, surprised.*

HELEN: Is that you, Sam?

SAM: What? Helen! Oh . . . I was miles away . . . what are you doing here?

HELEN: I'm collecting samples.

SAM: Look, I know I got drunk last night but isn't that a little over the top?

[HELEN *laughs and goes over to him.*]

HELEN: We're monitoring the seawater so we've got some evidence against the chemical plant. Not that it'll get us anywhere.

SAM: That's the trouble with multi-nationals. They don't have to listen.

HELEN: Aye. [*holds up the bottle and looks at the seawater*] Amazing, isn't it?

SAM: Looks like seawater to me.

HELEN: It's a lot more than that. It's life.

SAM: Yeah?

HELEN: You know that seawater has the same salinity level as our blood.

SAM: Really?

HELEN: All we did when we crawled out the sea all them years ago was bring eight pints of the stuff with us. And we're still pumping it round our bodies.

SAM: I've never thought of it like that.

HELEN: It's not just big and wet, you know. It's home.

SAM: And there was me wondering why I come and stare at it when I'm pissed off.

HELEN: So *that's* what you're doing here.

[SAM *looks away.*]

Tell me.

SAM: It's nothing.

[*He throws another stone into the sea.*]

HELEN: So who are you throwing that at?

SAM: I dunno. Me, I guess . . .

HELEN: And I thought *I'd* had a bad week . . .

SAM: What's happened?

HELEN: A big orange boat happened.

SAM: Ah. The one that takes men away and brings them back as heroes.

HELEN: That's the one.

SAM: And it's harder when you happen to love one of the men.

HELEN: Aye.

SAM: You know he loves you very much.

HELEN: Does he? He does everything with that boat. Paints it, cleans it . . . You know, if he could fit it in a cinema he'd sit on the back row with it.

[SAM *smiles.*]

SAM: It's not his fault. Dad's so desperate he follows in his footsteps that Luke doesn't know any other path.

HELEN: What is it with fathers . . . ?

SAM: Yours isn't so bad.

HELEN: When he was sober. About once a month I liked him.

SAM: Has it gotten that bad?

HELEN: It killed him. Last year.

SAM: I'm sorry.

HELEN: Don't be. By the end, none of us were.

[*Pause.*]

SAM: Get Luke off the boat.

HELEN: I tried. I couldn't even get him away from it for one night.

SAM: He doesn't belong there. He thinks he does, but he should concentrate on his carving. I saw that bird he did for you . . .

HELEN: I know. I never knew it was in him.

SAM: There's a side of Luke none of us knew. And it's the best part.

HELEN: Well . . . it's not my problem any more . . .

SAM: He's a fucking idiot.

[HELEN *is touched.*]

HELEN: It's good to talk to you, Sam. I was beginning to think I'd have to paint meself orange and have an aerial sticking out me head before anyone would listen.

SAM: It's good to talk to you.

HELEN: Except you haven't.

SAM: What?

HELEN: You haven't told me why you're throwing stones at yourself.

SAM: Oh, it's probably just being back here. Jo and Luke . . . so much bigger, braver, except nothing's really changed. Dad's still Dad and Mam's still stuck to him like a goddam barnacle.

HELEN: And have *you* changed?

SAM: I don't know. But I never belonged here. That's why I left.

HELEN: Looking for somewhere to belong? [*A beat.*] Have you found it?

SAM: Yeah. Maybe. I've found a way to reach people. And soon I'll reach thousands. Tens of thousands. One day, millions.

HELEN: That's what matters.

SAM: Connecting . . .

HELEN: Yeah!

SAM: Like the internet.

HELEN: All of us in touch.

SAM: Not just a crew, or a night shift, or a village . . .

HELEN: . . . but the whole world knowing enough about the rest of the planet to care.

SAM: Yes! Information is power!

HELEN: If people really knew what was going on they wouldn't let it happen.

SAM: But it isn't enough to just 'know', you have to 'feel' it.

HELEN: Or it's just news items.

SAM: A famine here, a plague there, an oil slick so far away it isn't real.

HELEN: It's the feelings that make the connections.

SAM: And that's where all the hope, all the possibilities, lie . . . in the connections.

HELEN: So where do we start?

[SAM *slowly moves forward to kiss her. She doesn't move away. He moves closer. Still she doesn't move. They kiss, gentle but lingering. She pulls away a little.*]

I shouldn't be . . .

SAM: I know. Neither should I ...

[*A beat. They suddenly kiss again, this time more passionately. Finally* HELEN *pulls away again.*]

HELEN: I should be going.

SAM: Please . . .

HELEN: [*looks at him*] Sam . . . you don't belong here. But I do.

[*She looks at him, kisses him gently again and then hurries away.* SAM *watches her go and then walks off in the other direction. As* SAM *leaves,* LUKE *backs onto the stage unravelling a large rope whose other end disappears offstage. The SFX of the sea continue.* LUKE *runs out of rope . . . it is stretched taut.*]

LUKE: [*shouting*] I'm there!

MIKE: [*off*] Now check it. There's a small cut in it some-where and I want you to find it.

LUKE: How d'you know there's a cut?

MIKE: I found it earlier.

LUKE: So why am *I* looking for it, then?

MIKE: I want to know if you can find it. It's all part of the job.

[JO *comes running up to* LUKE. *Without thinking, she holds the middle of the rope as she talks.*]

JO: What you doing?

LUKE: Wasting my time. What are *you* doing?

JO: The same. Mam wants you and Dad to come and have some chips by the jetty.

LUKE: What?

JO: She's got a strop on.

LUKE: [*weary*] Great . . .

JO: There's a cut in this rope . . .

[MIKE *enters.*]

MIKE: What's going on?

JO: Mam says you've got to come and have some chips.

MIKE: Chips?

JO: Yeah.

MIKE: Just chips. No fancy sauce or owt?

JO: Just chips.

MIKE: Marvellous. We'll be there as soon as we're done with this.

[JO *runs off.*]

JO: [*shouting*] By the jetty!

MIKE: [*to* LUKE] By the jetty? In this bloody weather?

LUKE: Mam's got a strop on.

MIKE: Find that cut sharpish.

[LUKE *starts to look half-heartedly.*]

It's the one we used for that cliff job last week. It got snagged when we were lowering the last one down.

LUKE: You know I couldn't have done that. I don't mind the sea, but climbing up a bloody cliff . . .

MIKE: Course you could, lad. You're made of the right stuff, you are.

LUKE: I'm a good crew member but that's me limit.

MIKE: Rubbish. You could be coxswain if you wanted.

LUKE: No way. Too much responsibility.

MIKE: Nonsense, lad. I've watched you . . . you're bloody good. You're like me. You care about that boat.

LUKE: Doesn't mean I want to run it, though.

MIKE: Course you do. It's in your blood.

> [LUKE *goes to where he knows the cut in the rope is and ties a knot there to show where it is.*]

LUKE: Here it is.

> [MIKE *is amazed and goes to check.*]

MIKE: You mark my words . . . ten years from now you'll be the best bloody coxswain we've ever had. Now let's go and get those chips.

> [*He begins to set off while* LUKE *coils the rope.*]

You know when I heard you sing the other night I thought to meself it's high time you joined the choir.

LUKE: [*calling after him*] Oh, Dad . . . not the bloody choir . . .

> [*He looks at the knot in the rope where the cut is. He is uneasy . . . he knows he conned* MIKE. *He shakes his head and slowly leaves. As he exits,* RUTH *enters, carrying a carrier bag full of bags of chips. The SFX of the sea continue.* RUTH *is on another part of the beach. She puts the carrier bag down carefully and looks out to sea.* JO *arrives.*]

JO: This is ridiculous.

RUTH: Just stop whingeing. It might not be Thailand but at least you're on a beach.

JO: Just hurry up with them chips. The sooner we've eaten 'em, the sooner we can go home.

> [RUTH *hands her a bag of chips and* JO *opens it and starts to eat.*]

RUTH: When do you think you'll go?

JO: Depends on the flights but I was thinking pretty soon. Before the end of the month.

RUTH: What about jabs? Don't you need jabs for them sort of places?

JO: I've booked 'em. For Tuesday.

RUTH: You're gonna be all right, aren't you . . . ?

JO: Damn right, I will. I haven't thought about it all these years to screw up now.

RUTH: Oh Jo . . . I'll not stop worrying about you . . . but I'm proud of you.

JO: Awww, Mam . . .

[*They hug each other.*]

And what about you?

RUTH: I tried. Last night. But he didn't hear me. [*A beat.*] He's been given the winch-man's job.

JO: What? That'll be another bloody ten years!

RUTH: I know . . .

JO: [*shouting*] Mam! You've *got* to tell him!

[MIKE *arrives.*]

MIKE: Tell him what?

[RUTH *looks away.*]

Well? What's going on?

JO: [*to* RUTH] Are you gonna tell him or shall I?

RUTH: Jo . . . please . . .

MIKE: Tell me what!

JO: I was just saying to Mam . . . when I get to Bali I want to meet a six foot four drug baron and have his love-child while trekking through Nepal.

MIKE: You what!

RUTH: She's *joking*, Mike . . . [*A beat.*] Aren't you, love?

[JO *glances despairingly at the sky.* LUKE *enters.*]

MIKE: So what *are* we doing out here? We're getting wet through.

RUTH: That's what you say on the boat, is it? 'It's started to rain a bit, lads, so we'd better go home.' We haven't been by the sea together for ages. I just hope to God we haven't left it too long.

MIKE: What the hell are you talking about?

RUTH: Shhhh. Listen!

[*They listen to the sea with varying degrees of commitment. Pause.*]

MIKE: So where's me chips, then? I'm starving.

[RUTH *hands* MIKE *a bag of chips. Then she holds one out to* LUKE *but before he can take it* JO *grabs it and kicks her shoes off.*]

JO: [*to* LUKE] You can't eat it till you're in the sea!

LUKE: What?

JO: [*pulling off her socks*] We're going paddling!

LUKE: Give 'em here!

JO: Come on!

[*She runs off, barefoot.*]

LUKE: But it's freezing in there. I know, I had to be 'man overboard' last week.

JO: [*off*] Come on, Luke. Your chips are waiting!

[LUKE *reluctantly takes his shoes and socks off.*]

LUKE: They'd better be worth it . . .

JO: [*off*] It's not so bad once you're in! You can hardly feel it!

LUKE: Aye. It's called frostbite.

[*He gingerly walks off.* MIKE *and* RUTH *watch, smiling.*]

RUTH: We didn't do so bad, did we . . . ?

MIKE: Daft buggers . . .

RUTH: *We* ate chips in the sea once.

MIKE: It was July. And I *still* felt daft. [*A beat.*] You were wearing that blue dress.

[RUTH *smiles. Long pause.*]

RUTH: Mike. They're going, you know. Luke's moving into his workshop and Jo . . . well, wherever she's going, she's going.

[MIKE *looks away.*]

Maybe it's time *we* were going . . .

MIKE: Aye. It's far too cold to be standing out here.

RUTH: No. I mean *really* going.

[MIKE *looks at her.*]

To where we paddled with chips.

MIKE: Cornwall!

RUTH: We could set up a little cafe and I'd do all the cooking . . . really do it, you know, like a proper chef . . . and you could hire out boats for the tourists. Proper boats, mind. We'd have to start small, just dinghies to start with, but we could build it up and between the two of us we could make a real living.

[*Long tense pause, then* MIKE *laughs.*]

MIKE: Daft bugger. Now I know where Jo gets her dreaming from.

[RUTH *suddenly pulls off her shoes and makes to run into the sea.* MIKE *grabs her and stops her.* SAM *enters, unseen by either of them.*]

What the hell are you doing?

RUTH: Mike, look at it! What do you see?

MIKE: Jesus Christ . . .

RUTH: Tell me! What do you see out there?

MIKE: The fucking sea!

RUTH: No! Look! There's Thailand. There's New York. Cornwall. Things that can be different. Somewhere else.

MIKE: You weren't *serious* about Cornwall, were you?

RUTH: I've been thinking about it for years. Planning, saving . . .

MIKE: Well, you didn't bloody tell me!

RUTH: Like you'd have listened!

> [MIKE *is thrown.*]

MIKE: What are you saying?

SAM: She's saying it's her turn to do some living . . .

> [MIKE *turns round, surprised.*]

MIKE: How long have you been there?

SAM: You're asking me a question?

MIKE: This is between your mother and me. You've no right to be –

SAM: You know, Dad, this is the first time you've looked me in the eye since I got back.

MIKE: What!

SAM: You haven't asked me one question. How I am. How my business is. How your son is. Nothing! And you've never wanted to know anything about me from the day I said I didn't want to go on the boat with you. Ten years! You haven't asked me a fucking question for ten years!

MIKE: That's not true!

SAM: When I call from New York you answer the phone and you say, 'Oh, hello. I'll just get your mother.' Not one word. Ever! All because I couldn't give a shit about the boat. And now you know I'm not the only one. You think they all love the boat the way you do? You think they've been happy? Their whole lives ruled by a boat? [*gestures at* RUTH] Every year she wanted to go away! Not just a weekend in Bridlington but a *real* holiday! And did you ever go? Never! What's it gonna take?

MIKE: I'll never leave that boat and you know damn well why!

SAM: Yes! I do! And it's bullshit! It's no reason to screw up a family!

MIKE: Shut it! You don't know what it's like to lose a father . . .

SAM: Yes I do.

[MIKE *reels, completely thrown.*]

MIKE: What have you ever wanted for, eh? All my bloody life I've worked for this family, gave you everything I could –

RUTH: Except time. [*A beat.*] All that time on the boat. Fixing. Polishing. Mending. Cleaning. Everything just right. But you've never given *him* that, have you?

MIKE: What the hell's going on round here? Suddenly the whole *world's* my fault!

SAM: You don't even know what the whole world *is*!

MIKE: All I know is I've spent me life rescuing people from that sea and now you talk about it as if it's some sodding *dream* land. Well, it isn't! It *kills* people! It killed my father!

RUTH: And if something doesn't change, it's going to kill us and all.

[MIKE *looks up at her, shocked.* LUKE *and* JO *come running on.*]

LUKE: I can't feel my feet! You've killed my feet!

[JO *laughs.* MIKE *sees them and leaves.*]

JO: You're soft! You can't take it!

[LUKE *sits on the blanket, desperately trying to rub some warmth back into his feet.*]

Typical man. All talk and no trousers. Hi, Sam.

LUKE: Trousers! It's a bloody wetsuit you need out there!

JO: Sam? You all right?

[*She becomes aware that something is wrong.*]

Mam? Where did Dad go?

SAM: Where do you think . . . ?

RUTH: It's time we went home.

JO: What's happened?

RUTH: Let's just get home, eh?

[*She clears up the mess on the beach and* JO *helps her.*]

Thanks, love.

[*They leave.* LUKE *watches them go, puzzled. The sea is still building.*]

LUKE: Sam?

[SAM *doesn't reply.* LUKE *is drying his feet and pulling on his socks and shoes.*]

What's going on?

[*Still* SAM *doesn't reply.* LUKE *gets up.*]

Well, I can't stay here chatting all day. Dad needs me at the boat.

SAM: No he doesn't. He just needs the boat.

LUKE: And his crew. I'll see you later.

[*He makes to go but* SAM *stands in his way.*]

What you playing at?

SAM: I'm not playing.

LUKE: I don't know what the hell's going on round here but I'm going to the boat.

[*He tries to leave again but* SAM *still blocks his way.*]

SAM: Where's Helen?

LUKE: I dunno. And she wouldn't care if I knew or not.

SAM: You should know. You should always know.

[LUKE *looks at him and then again tries to get past him.* SAM *stands firm.*]

Don't go to the boat, Luke. You should be looking for Helen. That's where you belong.

LUKE: What's she been saying? Have you seen her?

[*Suddenly a maroon goes off.* LUKE *looks up, startled and starts to run. But again* SAM *blocks him.*]

SAM: Don't go, Luke! He doesn't need you!

LUKE: What the fuck are you doing? I've got to get to the boat!

[*He tries to leave again and this time* SAM *grabs him.*]

SAM: No you don't!

LUKE: Get off me, Sam!

[*He pushes* SAM *down and runs off.*]

SAM: [*shouting*] If I loved a woman who kisses as beauti-fully as Helen . . . nothing in the world would make me get on that boat.

> [*Long pause.* LUKE *comes back. He looks stunned.*]

Who do you need, Luke? Who do you really need? Dad?

> [SAM *leaves. Another maroon goes off.* LUKE *falls to the ground, completely crumpled.*]
>
> [*Blackout. The SFX of the sea continue during the scene change.*]

Scene Five

Monday evening.

SFX: the sound of the sea fades as RUTH *is revealed in a pool of light. She is addressing the audience as if they were a meeting of the Women's Institute. She is wear-ing her Donna Karan suit.*

RUTH: I couldn't know when I said I'd talk to you that me husband would be in hospital. I'm sure you've all read about it in the papers. So I nearly didn't come tonight. But I did. For two reasons. Because the Women's Institute have always helped us, and be-cause the RNLI is about turning up.

You asked me here to tell you what it's like being a lifeboat-man's wife. I was gonna tell you about the friendships with other wives . . . it's not like other friendships. I was gonna talk about the funny times. Like when you're in the supermarket with your hus-band and a trolley full of shopping and the maroons go off and he runs out with the cheque book. And the car keys. I was gonna tell you about the times, that everyone wonders about, when the kids are out and you've made a nice dinner and put on them undies he likes and you're just getting started when suddenly he's off again, running to his boat.

But now there's been a trawler lost. Broken up by waves you and I can only imagine. All seven fisher-men dead. Seven men. Just gone. I remember me grandma saying that when she lost her husband in the First World War it wasn't hearing that he'd died that was the hard bit . . . it was living every day of her life without him. And now there are seven families who have to live every day without their husbands or fathers or brothers. Or sons. That's why we have to go on. Raising money, keeping the papers looking our way, and risking our *own* men. So thank you for asking me here tonight. Now if you'll excuse me I'm sure you'll all understand if I cut it short . . . I need to get back to the hospital.

[*She starts to leave, then stops.*]

Do you really want to know what it's like being a boat-man's wife? Do you? It may be scary when he's out there on a rough night, and you can never get it out of your head that he might not come back, but the really hard thing is knowing that when he rushes off it's not because someone else needs him more . . . it's because he needs *them* more than he needs you. And you can't say a word. He's a hero. Ask anyone. So you have to bury it and get on with it. And try to be grateful that, so far, you don't have to live every day of your life without him.

[*Pause. The pool of light fades to black.*]

Scene Six

Luke's workshop. Tuesday afternoon.

SFX: during the scene change we hear the end of 'Lying in the Sun' by the Stereophonics.

LUKE *is sitting, looking despondent.* HELEN *enters.* LUKE *looks up. They look at each other.*

LUKE: If you're looking for Sam, he's not here.

HELEN: I came to see you . . .

LUKE: Sam not good enough for you, either?

HELEN: What's he been saying?

LUKE: You go on about me choosing. Well, have you been choosing an' all? Between me and my *brother*? Or didn't you think you'd hurt me enough, thought you'd find another way to make your point?

HELEN: I didn't mean to hurt you. Just as you didn't mean to hurt me . . .

LUKE: At least I didn't go off with another woman!

HELEN: Might have been easier if you had. [*A beat.*] I kissed him. He caught me off guard. I didn't mean to . . .

LUKE: You've been drooling over him ever since he got here. I thought you were bigger than that, falling for all his bullshit.

[*A beat.*]

HELEN: So did I.

LUKE: Good, was it? Enjoy it? So how long's it been going on? 'Hurry up, Luke's in his workshop, we've got a couple of hours . . .'

HELEN: I kissed him. Once. I'm so sorry. I really am. [*Long pause.*] I heard you didn't go.

LUKE: . . . No . . . I should have. He needed me.

HELEN: What could you have done?

LUKE: I don't know. But he stayed out there too long, looking for the trawler. For those men. No one could survive in seas like that but he just kept on looking. The crew told him to turn back but he wouldn't listen. He got tired. Left the wheel. She turned beam-on. Should never let her turn beam-on in seas like that. He knows that! Seventh wave and over they went . . .

HELEN: Jesus . . .

LUKE: I should have been there. Then maybe he wouldn't have stayed out there so long. The crew were too frightened of him. Always have been.

HELEN: He'd have listened to you?

[LUKE *looks at her, hurt, defensive.*]

To anyone?

LUKE: Who knows . . . ?

[*Pause.*]

HELEN: Why did he stay out there so long?

[*Pause.*]

LUKE: Does this sound daft? I think he was looking for his dad.

[*Pause.*]

HELEN: Why didn't you go?

LUKE: It's not the boat I want to be married to.

[HELEN *looks away.*]

LUKE: I didn't *go* to the boat! Can't you see?

HELEN: [*wistfully*] Oh, Luke . . . [*looks at the heron*] You know herons don't migrate. They stay where they are. With their colony. They're beautiful and patient and strong. Like you. [*A beat.*] And they need the sea. It's their home.

> [*Pause. Then* LUKE *grabs his jacket and walks out.* HELEN *watches him go.*]

Scene Seven

The boathouse. Tuesday evening.

SFX: during the scene change we hear the sea and the tolling of a distant buoy.

LUKE *is revealed in a pool of light. He addresses the audience as if they were the crew of the lifeboat.*

LUKE: Before you all go I've got to tell you something. Tonight was me last training session. You see, I'm leaving the boat. I should have been with you that night. I'm sorry I wasn't. I let you down. And me dad. But . . . I realised something. That's why I was doing it. For me dad. I wanted to make him proud. But that's no reason to be here. Or to be anywhere. Whatever I do it has to be for me. So I'm leaving to find out what that is. You were the best crew ever. Still are. Not bad for a bunch of amateurs. But I've had some of the best days of my life with you lot. And I'll be thinking of you. Every time that bloody maroon goes off. Wishing I was there. And glad I'm not. Now . . . I think I owe you all a pint . . .

> [*The lights fade to black.*]

Scene Eight

The kitchen. Wednesday afternoon.

SFX: during the scene change we hear a solo voice singing 'Blow the Man Down'.

RUTH, *wearing an apron, is laying the table.* HELEN *is helping her.*

RUTH: Bravest thing he's ever done. I'm proud of him.

HELEN: Hope he hasn't done it for me. He'll resent me for it one day if he has.

RUTH: No. He loves you very much. But men don't leave their boats for women.

HELEN: Let's hope not.

RUTH: He did it for himself.

[*A beat.*]

HELEN: D'you think Mike'll go back?

RUTH: They won't let him. He's mine now. But instead of being full of the boat he'll be full of shame. Don't know which is better.

[SAM *enters brightly.*]

HELEN: Thought you were meant to go on Sunday . . .

RUTH: Changed his flight.

SAM: Wanted to make sure Dad was OK . . .

[RUTH *looks at him sharply.* SAM *goes to* HELEN *and shakes her hand.*]

It was good to meet you. Luke's a lucky man.

RUTH: Luke doesn't believe in luck . . .

[RUTH *leaves.* HELEN *breaks away from* SAM.].

HELEN: What the hell are you doing?

SAM: What's your problem? I got him off the boat, didn't I?

HELEN: You really believe that?

SAM: Just think . . . this time next year you'll be married to a sculptor. The kids'll never be short of wooden toys.

HELEN: If Luke and I get through this, it's no thanks to you.

SAM: Isn't it?

[HELEN *looks at him, hears* RUTH *returning and walks out.* RUTH *enters, carrying glasses for the table.*]

Well . . . the cab will be here soon . . . before I know it I'll back in the land of the brave and the home of the freebie.

RUTH: You going to keep pretending . . .?

SAM: Isn't it what we do? [*A beat.*] He wasn't there. We all lost out. And you let it happen. By pretending. By pretending we were all happy. So yes . . . it's a family tradition.

[RUTH *quickly moves to him and slaps him hard across the face.* SAM *doesn't flinch. He leans forward and kisses her on the cheek.*]

SAM: I love you too.

[*Pause.* JO *enters. She is carrying* MIKE*'s overnight bag and some flowers.*]

RUTH: Is he here?

JO: Luke's helping him out the ambulance.

RUTH: Oh, my Lord . . .

[*She dusts her hands and rushes out.* JO *eyes* SAM.]

JO: Still here, then.

SAM: I wanted to say goodbye.

JO: [*flatly*] Goodbye.

SAM: I hope Thailand's good. Watch out for the spiders . . . they're the size of dinner plates. And don't even think about going to Patpong.

JO: Will it be another five years?

[*She leaves through the door to the kitchen.* SAM *follows her off. We hear* MIKE's *voice as he enters.* LUKE, HELEN *and* RUTH *are trying to help him.* MIKE *seems older and smaller. He is using a crutch.*]

LUKE: There you go . . .

MIKE: Get yer hands off me. I can walk, you know.

RUTH: Now come and sit down . . .

[*She tries to help him sit down.*]

Would you like a cushion behind your back?

MIKE: I don't want no bloody fussing!

[LUKE *is now by* HELEN.]

LUKE: I didn't think you'd be here . . .

HELEN: Your mam asked me.

LUKE: Playing happy families, is she?

HELEN: Luke . . . she doesn't know about any of it. And she doesn't have to.

[JO *returns with the flowers in a vase.*]

RUTH: [*to everyone*] Now, I've made you a nice meal.

MIKE: Oh no . . .

RUTH: [*proudly*] Roast beef and Yorkshire pud.

MIKE: . . . Marvellous.

RUTH: With orange and coriander gravy. [*A beat.*] I'm only joking. The joint's in . . . it'll be ready in an hour.

[SAM *re-enters with his suitcase and laptop bag. He goes to leave.*]

MIKE: Didn't think you'd still be here.

SAM: I'm just going.

MIKE: You don't have to.

[*Long pause.* SAM *turns towards* MIKE. *Suddenly the tension is broken by a car horn.*]

SAM: Well . . . there we go. [*turns to* JO] Give my love to the beaches.

[*She looks away. He turns to* LUKE.]

See you little brother. Sometimes a little wobble's a good thing . . .

LUKE: Maybe. But as you said, I fall on my feet . . .

[SAM *turns back to* MIKE.]

SAM: Get better soon . . . [*looks at them all*] Well . . . have a nice day!

[*He makes for the door.* RUTH *suddenly rushes to him and holds him tightly.* SAM *can't hug her back because of the bags.*]

RUTH: Thank you for coming back for my birthday.

[*The car horn sounds again impatiently.* SAM *nods and then rushes out.* RUTH *looks around at her family. She goes through the door to the kitchen.*]

JO: So, how's your ribs, Dad? The doctor said that you have to –

MIKE: It doesn't matter what the doctor said. Me ribs are *my* business. If I want, I'll barbecue the bloody things.

[LUKE, JO *and* HELEN *smile.*]

JO: *You're* better, then . . .

> [MIKE *turns to* HELEN.]

MIKE: So I hear he's leaving the boat.

LUKE: Dad . . .

MIKE: [*to* HELEN] Happy now?

HELEN: I . . . I don't know . . .

MIKE: Well, you should be. You deserve the best.

> [LUKE *and* HELEN *look at one another.* RUTH *returns.* MIKE *turns to* JO.]

And what about you? You buggering off and all?

JO: . . . Next month . . . the flight's booked . . . Thailand, Kuala Lumpur *and* Bali!

MIKE: Sam gave you enough for all that?

> [JO *looks nervously at* RUTH.]

RUTH: . . . No . . . Sam's cheque bounced . . .

> [MIKE *laughs. His laughter builds. The others begin to join in. It becomes a huge release and lasts for some time.*]

MIKE: Bloody typical!

RUTH: So . . . the money I put aside for Cornwall . . . seemed a waste it sitting there not being used . . .

> [MIKE *nods slowly.*]

MIKE: Turn me back for five bloody minutes and the whole family does what the hell it likes . . . [*looks round at them all*] About bloody time!

> [JO *rushes round and, forgetting about his ribs, hugs him.*]

[*in pain*] Steady! Steady! Just watch out for them mosquitos. They're foreign.

RUTH: [*to* JO] Look, why don't you take Luke and Helen for
        a quick drink? I'm sure they've got lots to talk about.

JO: Fine. I love being the gooseberry.

        [RUTH *gives her some money.*]

RUTH: And buy a bottle of wine while you're out. Some-
        thing nice.

JO: OK. We won't be long.

        [LUKE *and* HELEN *are still lost in each other.*]

        [*as if to a deaf aunt*] We're going down the pub.

LUKE: Yeah? . . . Never say no to a pint. Let's go!

        [JO *leaves, followed by* HELEN. LUKE *pauses at the
        doorway.*]

        You know . . . we're better off out of it, Dad.

        [LUKE *leaves. Long pause.*]

RUTH: It's good to have you back.

MIKE: Just the two of us now.

RUTH: Jo'll be back . . .

MIKE: Not for long. Dreams in *her* head . . . we'll be nowt
        but a hotel. [*Pause.*] I can't stay here.

RUTH: We have to.

MIKE: No. If you've been saving for years you can't have
        given it *all* to Jo. We can still get to Cornwall.

RUTH: No we can't. You can't just give to one. So I gave
        Luke some towards his deposit for the workshop and
        Sam the same for his business.

MIKE: Then we'll find some more money, sell this place,
        sell whatever we have to. We have to get to Corn-
        wall!

RUTH: It's not about money any more. We belong here.

MIKE: I *can't* stay! I screwed up! Everyone knows it! How can I go to the pub, the bloody choir? What do I say to the crew?

RUTH: Listen to me, Mike. For once in your whole bloody life just listen!

> [MIKE *looks at her, startled.*]

We have to stay. If we ever leave, it'll be because we want to. If we run away now, you'll never be happy. All these years you've been brave enough to go out on that boat . . . now you've got to be brave enough not to.

> [MIKE *takes this in. He rubs his face, coming to terms with it. Long pause. He then tries to stand but the pain stops him.*]

Where you going?

MIKE: See how they're getting on with the boat. Must have been in a terrible state.

> [RUTH *goes over to help him up.*]

I can manage by meself!

> [RUTH *stands back.* MIKE *struggles to his feet painfully and slowly leaves. When she is alone* RUTH *goes back to laying the table. As she works, the lights slowly fade to black.*]

The End

Nell Dunn
Cancer Tales

Here are five women, each on a different and unique
journey through cancer. *Cancer Tales* takes us on an
inspirational pilgrimage of courage and despair,
love and reconciliation.

'These are moving, authentic voices, speaking from
real experience and real emotion. Nell Dunn has an
unparalleled ear for the speaking voice of emotion,
across the social classes. She treats an important and
painful subject with insight, dignity and bravery.
She is never sentimental, never alarmist, always true.'
– Margaret Drabble

'These stories illuminate the power that kindness
and humility have on those facing a life-threatening
illness and, indeed, on us all.'
*– Clare Moynihan, The Institute of Cancer Research
and The Royal Marsden Hospital Trust*

For a free copy of our complete list
of plays and theatre books write to:
Amber Lane Press,
Church Street, Charlbury, Oxon OX7 3PR, UK
Telephone and fax: 01608 810024
e-mail: info@amberlanepress.co.uk